I think when people say they are in love, they aren't sure. They assume they are because they have never felt these intense feelings before, or they certainly didn't feel like this in their past relationships. In my eyes, if you are willing to sacrifice everything to keep that person happy even if it means being at arm's length... then that's love. Nowadays, everyone has the want to need someone. Doesn't even matter what or who they are to them or how themselves are being treated, just as long as they are not alone. Being alone means everything gets real and they rather be with someone who fills that void for a while, then to find someone who can teach them the dark and light and build them up as a person. What hurts them is that when you're constantly in a toxic relationship, it's hard to see and believe when a person has real feelings for you. It's sad and it's no one's fault really. I don't think love is dead, but its reputation is.

- black sun.

Table of Contents

The Beginning

i. admiration

Late-night confession
My conscience you're blessing
Can't sleep on you
My mind needs resting
These petals could grow
We both can't see
At the end of the tunnel
We stand together free
Fascinated by your looks
But when it comes to your mind
It will never compete
You make me want to be serious
But laugh until it hurts
Travel with the kids
Talk over dessert
I envision a future with you
Different perspectives
Each one is perfect
Because me and you are connected
You reflect on me when you smile
I see a field of roses in your eyes
My heart is yours
You've branded your name deeply
No one had a chance before

- crinkles

Most of my time is spent on you
I've studied your little gestures
The way you pull on your ear when you're laughing
How you scratch your head when you're irritated
I admire you
And you don't even notice me
You tell everyone how everyone's the same
When I'm the complete opposite of you
If you only knew…
I'm a determined person
But when it comes to you
You've broken all of my rules
It's a one sided love
My whole demeanor changes when you walk in the room
Suddenly
I'm smiling
I've changed everything about myself so you can notice me walking by
And when you leave
I miss you
Even if I didn't talk to you
All this time I've been watching you
And I didn't even notice her watching me

- blind eye

The galaxy contains 100 billion stars
Yet, you chose me.

I want to meet you on the moon,
Hold hands with passion just like the sun.

Let the other planets be jealous of us.

- mars

I think my heart grew a couple of inches
I'm looking at you right now
I don't know if my mind is fooling me
But there are new discoveries every second
Of this journey together
All of the pieces are conjoining
Seeing the lights and exits
Every silent touch had meaning to you
Blind or neglect
This feeling was scary to me
I didn't have a dictionary or thesaurus
The web wasn't my friend
no cure
Just my trust and me
Wish us luck
And all I have is the past and present
So burying it is my safest option

- crush

Why is it that your eyes showed me such kindness?
That I can't forget that loving look you do
I tried my hardest to make you laugh
So I can hear and know your there
How is it that you're not affected when you let go of my hand?
You take a picture and I feel naked
I've forgotten all about the flowers and the field ahead of us
My view is just perfect
Looking at you

- seven wonders

I smile when you enter the room
You paint a picture so perfect
My favorite fragrance
I want to run away with you
Far from everything
Where I could only hear you and the trees
Your breathing is soothing for me to hear
Let the vibrations of your hums
Flow through both of my ears
I face all obstacles
You take away the fear
I'm invincible
You're the principle of everything I hold dear
Don't ever leave
I need you here.

- free

A night like this makes a person live and regret it the next day.

- phase

That smile is blinding
There are galaxies in your eyes
I think I'm seeing rainbows
Your halo is showing
I love hearing your voice
The way you express yourself
It's hypnotizing
Keep going
I have all the time on the planet for you
I'd move mountains on your say
And if you're sad
I'd grab the clouds to wipe your tears
Remember when I said
We'd rewrite history
Well I'd change the future
If it meant losing you
It isn't sacrifice to me
It is simply
Loving you.

- art

The angels in the sky fly high
That's where I see you and I
The soft cotton balls is where we lie
Until we depart
Then we will meet again in the stars

- dreams

She had a way with words
I questioned it because the expressions didn't
When we lived together
I thought every day was a fragment of what was to come

She kept quiet about her opinions
If she saw something unpleasant
You wouldn't hear about her unpleasant thoughts
Cursing was too much for her
It came with negative emotions

She never stopped asking for opinions
Cooking, clothes, watching documentaries
She always wanted to know what I was thinking

I could never tell her though
I didn't want to hurt her
I never did

- roommate

You had this beauty in a storm
You were different
Out of all the people I met
You were the one stuck in the back of my mind
I tried to forget you
It wasn't healthy to remember you
But I couldn't forget
I missed you when you departed
Everything began to feel cold
It's like when you left
All of these questions were left unanswered
I just had these floating memories
I should've said that I loved you when I first had a feeling
But I brushed it off
Too scared that I was going to lose you if I said it
And I did
I thought we had a good thing
You made me mad
But I made you crazy
You made me smile
I drove you wild
You reminded me of these flowers
They were gentle but they attracted opposites
I think they were daisies
We weren't made for each other
But I'd beat the odds to be with you everyday for the rest of my life
Even when I die
I always get this pain in my chest when I see you
Because I feel as if I'm not good enough
These insecurities haunt me
Maybe someone else can make your eyes crinkle from smiling

Or smooth out those wrinkles above your eyes
It was never that simple
That wasn't your cup of tea
You always fought against the system
You wanted difficult
You wanted the fear and the tears
The passion and the adrenaline rush
Even when I was never enough
You wanted me
I was your odd number
I was your person
I was the 1.

- numbers

I could write millions of words hearing your laugh
If it keeps that look on your face
Keep it on
It gives me reassurance
That life is worth it
As you are
Beautiful

- dependent

Let me pull the covers off
It's been too long since you've been recognized
I saw the sunlight leave from your canvas
Now all that remains are the shadows
I see the hurt in your eyes
You're crazy beautiful
And you're insane not to see that

Maybe you hide your strengths
It's been a while since you've shown it
Let me persuade you
Show you you're special
I promise you it's true

Whatever you desire
I will bring
You're sick of the world
I'll build a new one

We'll dance in the rain
Like the movies
Walk under the night sky
Our names will be significant
We're legends
You and I
Me and you
Sounds lovely.

- vision

You've thrown me off the ship
Slowing sinking into your love
No vest
I'm winging it
I see the Cupid's smiling above

- test drive

I've never fallen in love.
But I always believed I would.
Maybe once or twice
I would feel what everyone else talks or sings about.
I imagined it to feel like someone knocking on your door
First impressions
Hidden glances
Feeling the butterflies and blushes
And after you let them into your home
They begin to see more of your comfort zone
Your antics, your friends, interests
Everything is relaxed
Slowly your walls begin to knock down
There are some disagreements
But it isn't the end
Because you know you'll always come back to each other
And now when you try to cover up your dark side
It's shown in light
Your insecurities, perfections, and everything that makes up you
Slowly latches on to the visitor
And you find yourself falling deeper into their comfort zone
They keep breaking them down until there is nothing left
At this point, your home doesn't feel like it's yours anymore
It's just a nonessential thing
Just you and them now
Nothing to protect you
No more barriers or obstacles
You're just each other's shelter
And love is your protection.
But I've never fallen in love before.

ii. desire

Red curtains drape me completely when we fight
Orange in the fire we ignite
In the trees, I see green when we take our walks
The whiteness in your mouth when you talk
Blue like the ocean in your eyes
Brown reflects the honey dripping off your lips
Something that escalated turns into complete bliss
Even with the rapid desire
Time slows down
The world stops and the purple galaxy we are floating incomes around
You still grab the yellow stars just so I can see
The colors you give me

- rainbow

Late night rendezvous
Why another thought
When I'm thinking of you
The timing might be too soon

I am sure of the spark
This feel is too strong
I don't want to wait too long
What if this goes wrong?
I don't want to lose you
But I don't want half of you

The rush is too much
Heart is racing with just a touch
My head is filled with thoughts
Little Cupid's in the sky above
Pull back

I think about you until the sun comes up
Nervous
When I hear that raspy voice I always love
Music
My heart you're tugging
I need your comfort
Your actions say something
Why would I leave this
I need this.

- desperate

Looking at your lips
I feel high right now
Skies looking like the midnight sun
You're my type right now

- revelation

Grey clouds float in the Sky
Laughter engaged
The room gets bigger
It smells nice
I really love pie
Turning my head to the side
I see that silly smile plays on your lips
I know we'll be all right

It's something no one would miss
But right now it's just us
Spare the minutes
It might take a while but the heaviness of the effects
Might affect us right now
Something has to be done right now
It's hot right now
Maybe it's the leprechauns
But I crave you right now

Turning tables gives us the illusion we won't be able to leave this bed
So volatile, so gentle
Tangled bodies and words leave us a mess
And the way you're wrapped in that blanket
It's my favorite style
Nothing could be more perfect
And yet,
I still search for that smile.

- moments

Up high the smokes fly in the sky
Once I see that silly smile play on your lips
I know we'll be all right
It's something no one would miss
But right now it's just us
Just give me the time
It might take a while but the heaviness of the effects might affect us
right now
Something has to be done right now
I want you right now
Turning tables gives us the illusion we won't be able to leave this bed
So volatile, so gentle
Tangled bodies and words leave us a mess
And the way you're wrapped in that blanket
It's my favorite style
Nothing could be more perfect
And yet,
I still search for that smile.

-   simplicity

Be mine until the time runs out
Until the brown speckles fall
Releasing our Demons
Exploring our feelings
Touch by touch
It's enough
Talking is too much
Show me your pain
I'm seeing another world in your eyes
Different stars in the sky
The warmth of the sun
When you're wrapping me

Story of the century written here
Seeing a whole new you
I recognize you from my Dreams
Pink fills my heart
Delicate, gentle words and touches
You fascinate me
You are my favorite part
I won't ever let this go
Question is
Will you let this grow?

iii. pain

I floated in the sea
Deep in the water
You found me
I waited for you to grab my hand
You were so drunk sitting in the sun
You forgot how to stand
So I held my breath a little longer
Suffering in silence
I held hope
Losing time and space
I yelled within
Watched the bubbles form in front of my face
Never would I show discomfort
I was too dignified
I could hold on longer
I began to taste the salty metallic taste
Almost like pennies
It reminded me of my mother
She would always give me one
She'd tell me to go buy her a beer
I would walk to the store and grab two
One for her
One for me
Drinking one behind the counter
It tasted almost metallic
The bubbles
I would then run as fast as I could
Behind me were the muffled screams
It was then, I noticed
I couldn't breathe

- nightmare

2:32.
The exact time your face pops into my head.
The exact time I regret ever seeing you.
The exact time I hate myself for saying that.

- tick tock

Kind
Smart
Handsome
He is all of this
Yet I can't see past the minor errors
I'm looking for a wrong
But everything is right
I start a fight
So I don't have to spend the night

I lie
I hate
Only to push him away
Even if it puts me in pain
It's habitual
I wish I could stop
Maybe I'm still holding a grudge
I know this isn't love
It's just me being tied
I don't want to be inside
Somehow it feels safe
So I continue to play the game.

- quarantine

Midnight thoughts
Somehow you appear in my head
You have me writing little thoughts on the bed
I wish enough were said...

- reminder

I've tried hard to forget about the warmth you give
But when I do
I start to shiver
And I'm right back to where I started
Hiding behind your shadow
Thinking about you
words still not said.

- headache

You moving on didn't just make me angry
It made crazy, mad
Insane because of how fast it happened

It was like my love wasn't enough
The period of time in which we were combined was a test trial
And I guess that's what hurt me the most
You showing me that what I gave you
Someone else could
When in fact I gave you everything I had within me
And even beyond that
It was never enough
You wanted infinity
The whole universe
And I guess all I gave you was the world.

- quantities

I'm on my way
It's going to take some days
But I'll be there soon
Make sure everything is clean
I don't want to deal with your messes

-   dishes

He loved me forever
Time was never an issue
Until I stop showing
I thought what if I did show
Will it change things?
Or will my biggest fear come true
We'd stay the same
But the day never came
I shed a tear
For the potential future of us
Left in the rear
Out of town
I look down
I don't speak
I don't hear
I don't make a sound
The damage is already done

- welcome back

I check my phone every minute
Knowing damn well your name won't be on it
You don't care about me
You don't try to see
It's not making sense
Why I'm so lonely
I look for your shadows
Fighting what comes and goes
The different scenarios
Writing down which ones worse
Why I put you first
I wait for the key to turn
So I could confront the words you said
So I could confront the lies negotiated in my head
I'm trying to confront these changes
You're so fast to move
To see
You're leaving me
It's like I'm stuck seeing all the signs
I'm left behind

- notifications

Your perfect face doesn't deserve the tears I give you
Your perfect heart doesn't deserve the pain I put you through
How did I mess you up?
Everything I love
I corrupt
Blessings I wish never happened
I put you out in the open
Left you trapped
And then forgot about you
Now I'm writing
Praying you to forget about me too

- journals

I've spent years trying to fix this heart
I don't think I have all the parts

- repair

Maybe in a different universe
I'd choose to listen to you
But right now
My anger has blindsided me
It has already decided
I don't want you here
It caused us to be divided
And the shocking part is
I'm not completely opposed to the idea
My heart and body is too tired
I've lost all strength to go to you
So I choose to run
I want to latch so badly
But maybe this universe is against it
So maybe in another life
Another universe
I'll stay
And listen.

- dimensions

Take it back
Take back every word you ever told me
Every promise you said

- regret

The tattoos on my back
Tells me I can't get rid of you
The blood leaking from the crack
Tells me you'll break it again
I'll pull the knife out again and again
But it won't matter
You'll always be there to submit
And I can't pretend I'm the better one
Because I let you do it

- ink

My first love
I looked at you and everything froze
It's like I lost control
My hands started to sweat
I lost my breath
And in that moment
I saw something so strong
Through blurred lines
I envisioned a future with you

I didn't get a chance to use my head
My heart already chose you
You consume me
Through happiness
And my heart shattering
I still seem to smile when I hear your voice

I see the future and the flowers
Now you're saying you don't want that
You're giving up on me
And it's ok
I will pull through
Eventually
My heart wants you
but it doesn't need you

- garden

It's the heart that distracts you
While the mind plays tricks

- illusion

I've smoked plenty of times because of you
Wrote hundreds of rhymes because of you
Still won't donate any of my time for you
I know it's cruel
But I know you haven't thought of me too
I'm stuck in this yes or no game
I should just stop
Because in the end, I'll feel the same
I just want to know
So it can numb the pain

- antidote

You did give me the world
Just too small to fit the both of us

iv. reassurance

I'm in love with you
All the way.

How do you feel about that?
Is that something you'll consider?

- check box

Tiny flame in my heart
Do you love me?
Please do
Can't take it
If you won't
Convince me
Run with me
You've messed with my vision
Everything is much brighter
I'm appreciating the small stuff
Thank you darling
I was missing out before
Something beautiful just happened

- fires

Her heart was filled with summer rain
I used to put my hand on her chest to make sure she was real
That she wasn't some perfect joke.

- umbrella

-

I want to be the thoughts on your mind
I want to bring your whole world to a stop
What makes you smile?
I never want you to feel the same as everyone else
I want your words on the sky
Lie down and read them
When I look in your eyes
I feel your passion through my veins
I'll never be the same
A love is born
But it's been there forever
Perseverance through the pain
Ignited with a match
Started an explosion
Something I can't contain
Should I put it out?

- balance

I don't just want to hear from you
On the good days
I want you there on my rainy days
Holding the umbrella over me
Even when it's storming
I want you to walk with me and talk about the small raindrops
Because that's what real friendship is
Whatever status we're on
I want to know that we'll always come back to one another.

- rainy days

You didn't need me
That didn't stop me from needing you
I focused on the things you wanted
So I can adjust myself
Clueless
Foolish
I ignored it all
So why couldn't you ignore my flaws?

- birthmark

Writing down every moment just so I don't forget
Even though you tire me
I want your headaches
We've known each other for decades it seems
Moments of love, fights, lessons
You're finally on my team
It helps that we're the same person
Even when we don't want to be
Same thoughts run through our heads
Frightening that you could destroy me with a single word
I trust you so I know it won't happen
I want us to have years
Laughs
Ice coffee and tears
I'm smiling already

- houses and fences

If I help you out
Will you end my drought?
If I fulfill your needs
Will you help me plant my seeds?
It's all a part of different breeds
With the same means
I'm trying different places
Not trying to replace it
You need to face it
I need you
Will I see you soon?

- blind dates

It's been real quiet out here
Leaving this place alone
Pocket filled with tears
Shadow slowly disappears
I don't want to be lonely
Waiting for the warmth to hold me
The things you told me
On a loop for an hour
I don't think I know what this is
I don't think I could be fixed
Rather dismissed
I'm not in the mood for games
Time is running
Either we're both in or not
Not just one foot in
It's gotta stop

- games

I spend all day wondering if you have the same thoughts
Wondering if you're okay
Call me crazy
But when my phone lights up and I see your name
And when you talk about the things you love
It amazes me

- do disturb

No, I gave my heart to you
This is serious
I opened my mind and body
And gave you my heart and soul
Giving you
No
Knowing you have all the power to break it
I am risking the inevitable tears and pain that will destroy me
Just so I could live in this moment with you
So yes
I am in deep
The question is
Are you going to bury me?
Or jump in with me.

v. loyalty

Now you have to live with the burden of knowing you have someone's
heart in your hands
You're such a...
And I love you
Why would you do that?
You know what I've been through
I love you
And I hate you
I love you.

- frenemies

I write to forget you
To release into ink
It means you're not here anymore to judge my sins

Finding the meaning of this new life
Gets me through the dogfight
If I ask for strength
Would you give me it?
Or give me what's left of yours
True ones know the difference

Loyalty runs deep in the blood
We kill what we don't understand
And it's nothing but love
We let our patience test us
Our wars mean nothing
But a reference.

- gladiators

You support me at my worst
So I will be present at your best
Glass and sand can only reveal our enemies
The hidden sins
Not the ones displayed
We together stand on the tip of the mountain
Hand by hand we rein
Respect is admitting flaws
Not by the swing of their chains
We keep this embedded on our flesh
Standing together again we will remain.

- origin

My feet carry me even when my legs are weak.

My arms punch even when my muscles are strained.

My voice yells even when my throat is dried out.

My eyes stay open even when the tears try to drown its vision.

My ears hear every drop even when it sounds like explosions and gunfire.

My skin feels every blow even when the flame is blown out.

My mind races even when it throbs like the sound of a heartbeat.

My heart keeps forgiving even when it's shattered like the glasses underneath our feet.

My...

- the fight

There is nothing on this earth that has more love for him than me
Want to talk about sacrifice
I carried every burden on my back
Just to makes him feel less guilty
I dropped everything for him
I started to love the things that I once hated
And still, it's not enough
We were beautiful in the beginning
I thought he'd be my forever
My fairytale
My happy ending
I cleaned so perfectly so he can see I'm trying
I was so stuck on what I wanted
I didn't see what he wanted
And that didn't include me

It took years
For me to finally come into terms with it
So I'm here telling you
To treat him better than I ever did
To show him how to love unconditionally
To be his equal
To support him
Encourage him
And to never give up on him
Even when he hates you
Show him why he loved you in the first place
Motivate him to become a better person
And most importantly
Make sure he is so happy that he forgets about me.

- the talk

I hate it when you do stuff like that
You judge like you know what's best for me
You reek of criticism
But I'd change everything
If it meant losing you
You changed my personal beliefs
My faith
But it made me closer to you so I didn't lose much
I tried fighting this feeling
I tried to leave
But absence makes the heart grow fonder
And I tried to hate you
But at the end of everyday
You were there
And then I came to my conclusion
I rather hate you then anyone else

- revelations

My shadow lurks
I've seen you at your best
How I've been staring
I'm curious to where your flaws went
It's been driving me crazy how you've got nothing to say to me
Even though we aren't on speaking terms
I still send you goodnight and love you at 10:30 pm.
Can you blame me?
This wasn't the way I was raised
If someone hurt me, I stay away
I guess that's how much you've affected me

- sippy cup

Since I can't Face Time you
Will you give me the time to write to you?
Skype me so I can show you the stars too
Send me your number so I can count how many times you fascinate me
Call me whenever you need to rant or yell
And if a video or my voice isn't enough
And you want to see me face to face
I won't bluff
I'll travel miles to get to you
If you're into romantics
Then I'll throw pebbles at your bedroom window
Hold an old radio that plays your favorite tune
I'll even have food
It's a deal breaker
You'll have to let me in
It doesn't matter because I'll wait forever
Or at least a while
And I'll do all this
Just to see you smile

- just like the movies

I gave you everything
Anything you want

I let you see the stars
No matter how far
It's yours

I gave you everything
Anything you want

You didn't see the signs
You'll fall in line
In time

I gave you everything
And now what's yours
Is mine.

- legacies

I'm here waiting
Even when you mess up
I'm here waiting
Even when you yell at me to go away
I'm here waiting
Even when you undermine my ego
I'm here waiting
Even when you feel hopeless
I'm here waiting
Even when you break my heart repeatedly
I'm here waiting
I'm not going anywhere
You told me those 3 little words
You made a promise
Now you have to stick to that promise
You can't back out now
It's too late.
I'll be here until we're both not here anymore
Even then,
I'll still be here waiting forever
Because forever is a long time
And all I have is that.

- patience

We were walking side by side
Through heavy traffic
With the smell of New York lingering
I have a train to catch
You have a cab to catch
We never do what we're supposed to do

- crosswalk

The strength I give for the selfishness of your movements
It's not fair
Yet I stay here
Every game you win
Every flaw I see
You come back to me
I let you in
Some unjust spiral
I wanna leave
My heart doesn't have enough beats to see your tears
My brain could handle the fear
I could just run
But the memories overshadow
I'm back to square one

- levels

My heart told me it was you
My heart is the only thing pushing me through
It's the only thing that's convincing me to come back and scream
Just so you can hear me out
Because my brain disagrees
It hates you
It hates that you take up all of its time and space
It hates that you make my head hurt
It keeps telling me to give up on you
But my heart is telling me to run to you
I am trying to fight my head and listen to my heart
Because I believe that yours is saying the same thing

- vessels

When two souls interfere
There is no way they can disconnect
Despite any emotion
They come back to each other
Through videos in the mind
Or reminders in daily life
They are one

- doves

I find it hard to move on
When you're standing there
Makes me want to run back
Why does it feel so good?
I feel what you're doing to me
But I can't describe the feeling
It's a miracle
You're some kind of angel
I love all the attributes you give me
Adding more to my self esteem
I feel comfortable with you
The time moves so fast
And the way you laugh
Slows everything down
I'm trying to do the math
I come up with nothing
There's no way to explain how you love
It becomes complicated once we're stuck in the same place
Won't ever let go
We got the same taste
Found the same trace
You
I
Never replace
Why is this moving on thing taking so long?

- dark times

Today, I couldn't say I love you when you left.
You walked out so fast I couldn't even tell your shadow either.
I'll just try again tomorrow morning.

- trial and error

If I write about you
I won't ever stop.
It gets to the point
Where I am desperate to get you out of my head
I'd fight so hard to think of better things
But I come back to you in my darkest shadows
My demons love you
The angels hide from you
You don't make me feel alive.
In the end
It's just you and me
I don't know what else to do
So I let you win.

- K.O.

It's a void that goes deeper then before
The burn that never heals
When I open the door
It's empty
That's where you send me
Broken heart falls to ground
Cracking like porcelain dolls
It's where you left me.
There's no one else there who could help me
Put me back together completely and amend me
I'm stuck like this
But when I'm glued back
I fall for you again
There's only one you
I'm never going to learn
I am always going to reach for this flame
Even when it burns
I yearn
For the feeling of your fingertips
I yearn
For the feeling of your gentle kiss
I will always take the risk
And fall when I miss
Because when I'm lying broken again
There is where I will be lying for you
In complete bliss.

vi. closure

I love you
But I need to stop
Because you already did
And I think if we both move on
It won't hurt as much.

- tag along

You make me laugh
Smiles when your name comes up in a conversation
I giggle when something reminds me of you
Jump when I feel my phone vibrate
Thinking it's you that text me

You make me upset
Frown when your name comes up in a conversation
I look somewhere else when something reminds me of you
Lock my phone when I feel my phone vibrate
Hoping it isn't you who text me

- alerts

Give it my time
Let it waste all of my time
Give it my love
Make sure it is enough
Give it my heart
Let it tear me apart
Give it my tears
Clean what was there before?
Give it my laugh
Something for it to adore
Give it my pain
I won't pride
I've done enough damage
Put you aside
Now you have a better life
I'm alone
So there's no one left to hold
I'm cold

- sweater weather

I ignored the secrets you whispered in bed
When you thought I was asleep
Nothing but radio silence at the table
Hidden clashes in between
Cried enough rivers for you
Yet no teardrops for me
Maybe there's something I'm missing
Maybe there's something I can't see
Constantly I give you my diary
Even left you a spare key
I keep giving and giving
And you're already ready to leave
I think it's time to start another chapter
Let myself be free
Hopefully when I'm ready in the future
I can give my book to someone else to read

- paperwings

All the good things are bad to you
I think you got that from your mother
Nothing's enough
Never look on the bright side
Even though I try
I'm not perfect enough for you
It gets tiring
Trying to stitch the cut
So you can't see
Even when it's hurting me
I'm getting frustrated
Making sure you have all you need
Each second changes
You could never put together your thoughts
I had to do it for you
Knowing this was your fault
This was already lost
Same thoughts in my head
I prayed to forget them
The feelings dead
Constantly fighting
Even though enough has been said
I love you has been worn out
Won't stop the drought
This was done
Our time ran out

- stop the watch

The kind I want to laugh with
The kind I want to dance with
The kind I want to run with
The kind I want to show off
The kind I want to meet my family
The kind I want to blush about
The kind I want to smile about
The kind I would give my heart to
The kind I would get jealous for
The kind I would sacrifice for
The kind I would fight with
The kind I would have my heart broken for
The kind I would cry for
The kind I would miss.

- the kind

New beginnings
But you're stuck in the past
I meet someone new
You get mad
I can't help it
I want more than this
You're criticizing
Something I won't miss
Everyone else doesn't carry this baggage
Whatever fear you're packing
Keeps us from moving
Instead, we're lagging
It's time to give it up
We're not healthy
Bickering, not listening
We used to be so lovely

The End

To my past, present, and future. And to Jenni, I owe you the universe.

CPSIA information can be obtained
at www.ICGtesting.com
Printed in the USA
BVHW011752200421
605394BV00009B/1719